I0430186

How To Write a Book

The System

by Dan Moskel

This publication is designed to provide accurate and authoritative information in regard to the subject matter covered. It is sold with the understanding that the publisher and author is not engaged in rendering legal, accounting, or other professional services. If legal advice or other expert assistance is required, the services of a competent professional person should be sought out.

ISBN-13: 978-1499640564

Printed In The United States of America

Contents

Chapter 1. Introduction

How awesome will it feel to add to your resume, that you're published author?

How about being able to say to your friends, family, and associates, they can grab a copy of your book at iTunes, Amazon, BarnesandNoble.com, on the Kindle, Nook, and in audio book?

How cool will that be?

The best part about writing a book, is this is a great way to generate passive recurring steams of revenue in the form of royalties on your book sales.

Would your life improve with multiple recurring, passive streams of income?

Could that help you break free the bonds of spending Monday through Friday with Dwight Schrute and Michael Scott from the hit TV show, The Office?

Let me share a cold harsh reality, it's said 8 in 10 Americans want to write a book, but how many of these well intended folks, actually do it? The Department of Labor in 2012, reported less than 130,000 writers and authors, among a population of more than 300 million people. In other words, the odds are about as good as winning the lottery.

The plain truth is writing a book, is a job. It requires you to invest energy, time, and effort. But, it doesn't have to be some long arduous journey.

If you listen to what the others say, you'll hear them yammering on about investing years into writing a book, and how painful the experience is. Recently, I even heard one author say he had two major illnesses, two surgeries, and spent two years writing his book, and still has no idea what to do differently, other than purchase better health insurance for the next one.

Come on man, how about trying anything differently!

You see the Rosetta Stone to writing your book is following a simple, proven step by step formula. This is how you write one book and if you so choose, five more, and without feeling like your donating an organ, giving birth, or solving advanced calculous.

Surely, you've seen an episode of the hit TV show, Shark Tank, with Barbara Corcoran, she's written three books. But, did you know she has dyslexia, and was a D student in high school?

It doesn't require a Harvard degree, and the lack of a formal education didn't stop Charles Dickens, H.G. Wells, Jack London, or Mark Twain, to name but a few!

Look, this is my eighth book, and just like Chris Farley, in the movie Tommy Boy, I barely escaped college, in less than a decade, and started writing professionally as a college dropout. During our great recession, and have earned millions of dollars, working from home, and even part time, while finishing school.

You may have even seen me on national TV in my own infomercial. It's awesome to say I've appeared on ESPN with LeBron James, even if we weren't playing basketball together. I don't say this to brag, but so that you will take my words seriously.

In this book you'll be empowered with a simple, bite size, 11 step system to become one of the few brave courageous souls, that takes this dream, and turns it into a reality. You are a dreamweaver, let's get busy and make it happen.

Just think about what being a published author, will do for your career?

Surely, it'll pour rocket fuel on positioning you as an expert, and authority in your field. Along with raining down upon you potential media interviews, speaking engagements, new clients, the sky's the limit.

Do you hear that knocking?

For it's the moment of opportunity at your door. But, just like in the movie the Matrix, Keanu Reeves was given a choice of the red pill or the blue pill, right now, this moment, you're faced with the same decision, what choice will you make?

You see, it's not luck, happenstance, or black voodoo magic that you're hearing this message.

Come, along now. Let's get started with step #1, and the very first place to start, and keep in mind what Mark Twain said:

"Twenty years from now, you'll be more disappointed by the things you didn't do, than by the ones you did do."

P.S. Please, grab your bonus "peek over my shoulder" videos at DanMoskelUniversity.com, and get your free gift of the 7 weapon book marketing tool chest and check out the full details about a free media interview to help create this surge of interest in your upcoming book publication, limited to the first 1,000 respondents and new authors.

Chapter 2. Before You Write a Word

Writing a book is like running a race, it's not about how fast your start, or how slow you go in the middle, the only thing that matters is crossing the finish line. For our purposes, the finish line, is publishing, everything else is merely window dressing.

Game Plan

The very first step is to create a plan, just as the wise Ben Franklin and Winston Churchill said: "If you fail to plan, you're planning to fail." You see, most folks know this and start by planning out their book, but this is the forsaken path to feeling overwhelmed, frustrated, and the pipe dream of achievement.

Listen, to what Jim Rohn says, an early mentor to Tony Robbins, and give yourself reasons to write your book. Please, take a few minutes and the very first place to start is by jotting down a few detailed reasons, why you want to follow through on this goal, and what it will mean to you, your loved ones, and how your life will change?

This doesn't have to be an exhaustive time consuming process, but do invest some time with it, because you'll want to look at this reasons list, every single day. The objective here is to make measurable progress in reasonable time.

Timeline

The second step is to give yourself a timeline. This is simply a general idea, of how long you plan and expect it to take to write your book.

There are no rules. And many great books have been written in just weeks, including A Clockwork Orange, also made into a movie. The Strange Case of Dr. Jekyll and Mr. Hyde is said to have been written in less than a week. But, Ray Bradbury has the best story of escaping two noisy kids and renting a typewriter at UCLA, for 10 cents an hour, and writing Fahrenheit 451 in only nine days.

I'm not suggesting you need to write this fast, but do give yourself a general idea of how long you expect this process to take. Include milestones as well, such as your first draft completion, editing, and of course, write down the finish line day for when you plan to be a published author with your book available for purchase!

You see, this is a lot like writing a paper in high school. The teacher gives you an assignment with a due date of next Friday, and if your anything like me, you go play until Thursday night, and have that O shoot moment, and frantically go run off to stay up half the night.

The big difference here however, is rather than get an arbitrary grade, you get money for your work!

You see, another big stumbling block, is not planning breaks. This is not an overnight process. There's a lot of moving parts, and it's important to give yourself, and your mind, some periodic planned time away.

You'll have to exercise self discipline, take action, and follow through with completing your assignments. After all I've yet to hear of positive thinking writing a book, or Donald Trump say it's the key to constructing magnificent sky scrappers. And just as a wise man once said procrastination is a lot like masturbation: "In the end, you wind up just screwing yourself."

Look, this process is simply writing a few papers, and then combining them to make a manuscript. And just like when you're a kid and you waited until Thursday night, you'll have to get tough with your time. When you plan to work, get busy. You can't let Trudy interrupt your focus, with her latest Facebook post, or a text message from Laura telling you how she can't believe Becky said her butt looks big! This is one reason why so many people go through life, with merely the pipe dream of writing a book.

You also need to find your ideal working environment. No two of us are alike, and you may have to try a few places, but you need an atmosphere where you can work, uninterrupted, and really focus. This is a job, and you'll have to put in effort, but don't let the herds view of this so called "hard work" stop you. And remember, it if were easy everyone would do it!

The Journey of Cervantes

The famous author of Don Quixote, Cervantes, who by the way survived 5 years in slavery, is famous for saying: "The journey is better than the inn." And how true it is!

You see, the point here is you have to relax. This is a journey. It will take some persistence, commitment, and follow through on your part. But, it's worth it, and one of the keys is to keep your list of reasons at the top of your mind, use this as the jet fuel to help you along, especially if you hit a few potholes.

The key is to avoid feeling overwhelmed. Be flexible to adjust, and give yourself extensions, if you need a few. Your objective is to remain calm, cool, and comfortable, not only do these feelings flow into your writing, it is vital to avoid investing years, risking a major illness, and panicking about this project.

You see, it needs to be as easy as possible, and if you enjoy this journey, you will write a much better book. It's like public speaking, when someone is visibly nervous, it detracts from the message.

It's essential that you set things aside and take a systematic step by step approach to this goal. Break it down into bite size, pieces. Many folks get stuck waiting to come up with a perfect title, or a majestic beginning, to get started.

The Trump Card

Listen, when your feeling those creative juices flowing don't hesitate to play the trump card, and just write. A big challenge is getting these magnificent ideas out of your head and into tangible words, so anytime your feeling in the zone, run and run fast with it!

Coach John Wooden

Avoid the trap of perfection, this is not a worthy goal. Instead aim for excellence. NCAA Hall of Fame, head coach, John Wooden led his basketball squad to win 10 national championships in 11 years. At one point they won 88 straight games, over 3 years. Coach Wooden said:

"Success is peace of mind, which is a direct result of self-satisfaction in knowing you did your best to become the best, that you are capable of becoming."

You see, there is a natural evolution to writing a book, and so long as your moving toward the finish line, and have the courage to cross it, and publish your book, you're successful and among a very small percentage of people, a published author.

Just as coach Wooden would say no two of us are alike and we all learn in different ways. This book is the ingredients and the recipe, but I must admit, you'll likely have to tinker a bit to find the exact amount of each ingredient that works best for you. I continue too tweak a few things, and have discovered some projects require a little more here, and a little less there.

As long as you cross the finish line, and publish your book, I'll be left satisfied and smiling. If along your journey, you discover a breakthrough technique that helps you cross the finish line, please give me a shout, so I can share it with the others. You'll receive full credit, of course, and a plug for your book, I can be reached at:

Dan Moskel
803-422-5795
dmoskel@gmail.com
http://www.danmoskeluniversity.com

Step #1 - Wrap Up

At this point you should have your reasons list, this is how your life will change when you become a published author, along with a game plan and a rough idea of how long you expect this project to take. Avoid paralysis by analysis, stay calm, cool, and collected, in order to do your best.

Chapter 3. Build a Swipe File

In this step were performing the research. Your "swipe file" is like a brain storming session. You just want to write down everything you can about your topic.

Write down stories, keywords, ideas, sentences, you name it. The more you get out here, the easier step two will be, right now just write, the only wrong answer is not writing!

You see, this will help formulate the contents of your book, giving you ideas, topics, chapters, and sections you want to include. I suggest you start right where you are, and then we will discuss a few tools to use in this process, to help, especially if you're still choosing a topic.

From time to time, you'll benefit by going back through these steps, with this project, and any subsequent books you write. It's my priority that you use this information, as a reference guide to writing your first book, and your 14th best selling book.

Your swipe file, is an idea dump. You want to get all the stuff about your topic into a central location, start with everything you know. You'll have to do this at some point in the process, it's most efficient to do it first, this will make organizing your work, and the flow much easier.

Once you've gotten everything you know out on to paper, you'll benefit by using these four tools to continue and build out your swipe file, and make sure you've gotten everything you want to include. These four tools will also help you determine how big your market is, and provide you with useful insights about your reader. Along, with information about how to best structure your book, to make it most appealing to your audience, but one step at a time.

4 Tools

1. Other Books

Continue reading. It's a good practice to go and skim through some of the popular books within your topic. This will help give you ideas, sub topics, chapters, and even some organizational thoughts, about how you want to structure and share your message. It's key to hook your readers right away, or else they may never get through your book, but more on this in a bit.

You see, by going and looking at what currently exists in the market on your topic, you get to see first hand what's available to your target reader. You may want to visit the local bookstore, and go online. Take note of any good items, or anything you forget and write it down on your swipe file. If you don't write it down you'll lose it, trust me, I speak from experience.

Brian Tracy says to get the top 10 books on your topic and read them. But, other authors say it's best to avoid reading books on your specific topic, while writing yours. I personally recommend reading related information about copywriting, communication, and interesting stories. I'll often find neat anecdotes, to share in my books.

2. Magazines, Newspapers, Websites ...

You'll need to immerse yourself in the information that currently exists about your topic. This is also useful in finding supporting documents, quotes, research, and even just good ideas to include, and see what is interesting to other people within the existing body of work.

For example:

If you're a therapist writing about ADD it's be a great idea to take note of some of the conferences, medical associations, existing websites, and articles. This helps you to really see your topic from the eyes of your reader, and target audience.

Along with possibly shifting your focus. You may notice there is a limited amount of information available on Adult ADD, and this may be a market you should target, after all the research shows only 4.1% of adults 18 to 44 years old suffer from this, compared to 7.5% of kids.

You'll also benefit by taking note of some of the leaders in your market. These folks may be very helpful to reach out to, and ask for help with creating a stampede of folks running to purchase your new book. Along with possible media appearances, interviews, speaking engagements, and platforms to spread the word about your upcoming publication.

It's equally important to gather a few things you want to avoid with your book. You must strive to make your message unique and written in your true voice. Please, avoid trying to copy the existing research by simply putting into your own words and the false belief that people will be interested in purchasing it. Your book must be different, and unique.

3. Google Keyword Planner

This tool will briefly require you to put on your pocket protector, but I guarantee it will be worth it. You see, this one tool, will give you some reliable data on the size of your market and more, but let's stick to one step at a time.

The Google Keyword Planner is an advertising platform, and yes with Google. This is a free tool. You'll need to visit Google AdWords to sign up.

The value with this tool, is you can see the exact number of times people search in Google for a specific keyword term. The idea here is to discover:

• The size of your market

Generally speaking, the more often your topic is searched for, the bigger your market. You may also discover there isn't much search volume for your topic and you may have narrowed it down a little too far, or vice versa.

• Chapter Ideas and additional topics

It also gives you good ideas for related sub topics that people are interested within your general topic. One such example is with a book of mine "Email Marketing That Works … So You Don't Have To" some of the high volume or commonly searched keyword terms include:

- Email marketing campaigns
- How to build an email list
- Email marketing services
- Email marketing examples

This is good information to use when creating chapter titles, and headings in your book. The objective is to get a better understanding of the concerns that are on your readers mind, speak their language, and to speak to your audiences top priorities and concerns.

We want a big general market, and then a segment (sub set) inside that market. Your book can't be written for everyone. If you don't heed this advice, it will be written for no one.

Key points:

If you choose to self publish your book, you'll need to use some keywords to help with the listings at online retailers. You see, just like people search in Google for information, they also search in Amazon. And if you choose high volume search terms, your book, can get listed in prime positions to get more views, which should translate into more sales, and cha-ching more royalty payments. Take note of the top five to seven keywords, write them down somewhere, you'll need it again, if self publishing.

In sum, this tool is priceless, and an effective way to give your book topic a quick evaluation to make sure there is a market for your information. I know it's a bit like math, there are numbers involved, but it can translate to numbers in your bank account. And money math should be automatic even if your like me, and advanced calculus will always be a dream of abilities, that I slept through having.

4. Your Audience

The last tool for creating your swipe fie is becoming one with your audience. I'm not suggesting you go trying to sleep with people, claiming you're doing research for a book, but that doesn't sound like a half bad, method for a single guy like myself.

Your objective here is to put yourself in your readers shoes, and try to see their world.

- What is their typical day like?
- How do they spend their time?

You want to get in their mind and try to become one with them. Write down a few details about your ideal reader, the more specific the better.

We'll dive into this in some more detail coming up, but right now, it's good to get a mental picture and understanding of who your "perfect reader" is EXACTLY! This is going to personalize your message, and assist you in keeping your reader hooked, interested, and hanging on every word you write.

- What are their top 5 concerns?
- Life goals?
- What keeps him up at night?
- What are his insecurities?
- Interests?
- Hobbies?

This is a good exercise for every piece of communication you create, and enables you to speak to your audience and have an intimate conversation with a friend. You're the friend that understands.

For example:

With the topic of how to build a website, the first book I wrote. There are two very different and distinct segments in this market. On the one hand their is the uber geek like Screech from Saved By The Bell, and then their is the baby boomer retiree and non tech savvy guy just looking for an easy website, after all we are in 21st century, right, it's not rocket science?

But both these groups are looking for vastly different material inside the same general topic. You can't write to both of them, and if you try, you'll loose both. This is why you must narrow down and choose your reader, and the segment of the market, you really want to target.

I've even heard book publishers targeting parents, they believe will buy children's books, and that's pretty darn intelligent if you ask me! Please, don't neglect this, step.

You should have a good swipe file after exhausting your mental powers and using these four tools! Take a breather, and swig some water, because coach wants you back in the game and to take a look over your piece of paper, or rather papers, plural. The goal is to get one centralized location of all relevant information and ideas you want to include in your message.

This swipe file is the foundation for your book. From this one exercise everything else will grow and blossom. You're like the farmer, tilling the soil getting ready to plant your crop!

Step #2 - Wrap Up

Right now, you should have a big piece of paper or four pieces of paper, with a whole bunch of stuff written on it. My files will often contain random notes written in diagonal, vertical, horizontal, and important things circled and underlined. It looks like an unstable guy's random thoughts and gibberish, but that's okay. As long as I know what it means. And as long as you can interpret your swipe file, a little temporary embarrassment hasn't hurt anyone.

Last Word

Relax, your ideal reader maybe George Castanza from the TV show Seinfeld. Who know's you maybe having an intimate conversation with him in the restroom, and not even know. Please, have fun along this journey, it's exciting!

Chapter 4. Let's Make an Outline

These initial steps are time consuming, but it will make writing your book much easier, and you'll work exponentially more efficiently. Trust me, you'll wind up going through these steps regardless, it's better to do it now, than halfway through your book, which often results in a jumbled, overwhelming, frustrated, mess. Feel free to try it that way, but do it on the second book you write, for now, just hang with me.

Now that you have your swipe file, with all the ideas, and topics, you need to do an initial breakdown. The objective here is to start clumping related information together, along with building the big picture outline for your message.

The end goal, is to break your book up into chapters, sections, and even random items you want to include. You'll need to rinse and repeat this process, most likely a few times. To clarify, don't go all out here, but do go through and start putting related information together. If you have some ideal chapters or sections, by all means run with it. This doesn't have to be perfect, and there's no rules, but this is the first step to organizing your information.

The Structure

Listen, as a author, you're now an architect. You've got to engineer a book that is engaging, and interesting so your reader will keep flipping the pages. The plain truth is, many folks don't read books they buy, nor use products they purchase. I've done it myself! If a book isn't keeping me entertained, I toss it aside, almost never to return.

Have you too done this?

You see, you want to create a structure that is gripping, entertaining, and leaves your reader wanting more, more, and more of you! I suggest, you try thinking about it, if the two of you, you and your ideal reader, were hanging out for a weekend at a lake house.

- How would you go about sharing your material with him?
- Where would you start?
- What would you say next?
- What sequence of events is most compelling?
- What will hook him into your book?

This is just like preparing a presentation, but without the public speaking. I like to picture gathering up all the little ones and sitting in a circle to tell a story. You gotta keep their interest, or the'll be off in a flash, trying to ride the dog again, and sticking crayons up their nose.

You see, the structure is just choosing a path, there are a million different paths and ways to present your information. But, you must choose one way, there is no wrong way. It's also important to know, these decisions aren't locking you in. You can always change the sequence later, if you decide there is a better path. But, it's good to get an initial blueprint together, now.

Book Outline

In a perfect world, you'll be able to break up your book into a nice neat, set of 12, 18, 21, chapters, but that's probably not reality. You've likely divided up some chapters, and have an idea of the structure, but there are a few random items left about, and that's okay. The plan is to break this book up into bite size chunks. Then, we'll create an assignment with a deadline, for each specific chunk, or chapter for your book.

For example:

Let's say you have 12 chapters, now if you'll just focus on writing one chapter, and give yourself a deadline of one week for example. In three months, you'll have written the meat of your book. It's key to focus on one topic at a time with your writing, it's easy to get distracted by the million little things, and wind up feeling overwhelmed and ill.

It isn't easy, and you do have to get decisive, along with having faith in yourself. It's important to keep tabs on your specific style, for me, I need a set of clear, simple, steps to follow. I bet, this is why it took me almost a decade to graduate college. We have to make this project, manageable and easy. There are many folks, including one of my favorite authors Dan Kennedy, who didn't even attend college, and he's written dozens of books.

In addition, with the beginning, introduction, title, and any other details, I'll often set those aside and at most jot down a few notes. The most challenging part of this project is turning your ideas and thoughts, into words on paper.

Deadlines

Yes, it's a dirty word, but don't go scurrying away like my 3 year old nephew, he's still scared of the dark too. I suggest you view deadlines, exactly like a paper in high school, and I can relate if high school doesn't bring back all pleasant memories, I attended five.

This time around, you get money for your papers! But, look it's human nature to put things off until Thursday night when the assignments due on Friday. This is why it's said, you have to make yourself attractive to success and wealth, instead of chasing it.

Go back and grab your game plan from step #1, how long do you expect this project to take?

Do you need to make any adjustments, now that you have a better idea of how much work you'll need to accomplish?

Schedule

Now were going to set up your schedule. This is the idea, we want to set up the easiest, simplest, smoothest path to persist and accomplish this goal, so you will cross the finish like, and publish your book.

Let's look at how to do this.

Let's say you're giving yourself roughly 90 days to write your book. Now, go and look at your outline how many chapters do you have roughly, 15 for example, plus some random items. Awesome, let's go ahead and call it 16 chapters, so we'll have time to write the random stuff. And let's plan two breaks, to be reasonable with ourself, and that will make 18 chapters. Here comes the math, were going to take our 90 days, and divide it by 18 chapters, that will give us five.

This schedule will require writing one chapter, every five days. Along with giving us two breaks, each five days long.

• Is that a sustainable schedule for the next 90 days?

Do you see how this works?

The objective is to make it EASY! Please, plan breaks, and this schedule is just for writing your manuscript. You'll have to invest time editing, writing an introduction, a title, and a bunch of little details, but writing the content, and getting the message out is a big stumbling block. Be flexible, on your journey to make adjustments if you need too, and be disciplined to turn that paper in, and make a book! After all, you get a return of royalty payments, and money!

A favorite quote of mine that always keeps me moving forward is from Dan Kennedy who says:

"Writing a book doesn't have to take a long time, nor should it. Writing slow only earns you less money."

Step #3 - Wrap Up

At this point you should have a schedule that's broken up your book, into small bite size assignments. In addition, to a working outline, with some ideas on the structure and sequencing of your material, and how exactly you intend to share your message. Stay relaxed, and focus on doing your best, making measurable progress in reasonable time.

Chapter 5. Keep Em Reading - 6 Winning Writing Strategies

Look, right now you should be feeling empowered, and ready to conquer the world. You just turned a mountain into a molehill of bite size manageable assignments, with a schedule to completion! Just as Rome wasn't build overnight, neither will your book be, but it will be constructed and that's all that matters.

In this step, we're going to review six winning writing strategies. This is what makes your book stand out, strike a cord with people, and sell, sell, sell.

1. Be Like Cleopatra

You've surely heard the story of Cleopatra, and how she was able to seduce powerful rulers in the Roman Empire including Julius Cesar, and Marc Antony. This is how Cleopatra was able to seize and hold power over ancient Egypt.

Your book needs to follow this same strategy. You need to seduce your reader, to keep them flipping the pages, to consume your book. After all, you're not writing it, so it can go collect dust, you want people to actually read and benefit from your material. The best piece of advice I've heard is: "Each word, should sell the reader, on to reading the next word."

- Let me ask you, what's the best book you've ever read?

- And what made it so spectacular?

I'll bet it's a book that reached out and grabbed you by the shirt lapels and just like me, kept you hanging on every word, as if you were one of Pavlov's dogs hearing a familiar ringing. Just look at the way we describe a good book to our friends, we say: "It was so great, I just couldn't put it down."

This is what you want people to say about YOUR book! You want people to be so consumed, they fell compelled to stay up late, and keep reading your material! This principle is true of every type of media: movies, TV shows, magazines, newspapers, you name it.

The deadly sin, you must avoid is being BORING! The last thing you want, is your reader to feel, as if their listening to the Ben Stein character, in the movie Ferris Bueller's Day Off, as the teacher asking the class for the umpteenth time: "Anyone … anyone?"

2. Frustrate Your English Teachers

Did you know the average American reads on a 6th grade level?

GASP … it's true. A colleague and friend, Perry Marshall, says he puts all his writing though a program to make sure he's writing at a 6th grade level. By the way, Perry is the author of nine books now, and a leading marketing consultant charging clients $2,000 an hour, and prior to this he was building a tech company that sold for $18 million.

Listen, your number one goal is getting your reader to understand, and comprehend your message. This is a law, true of all types of communication: print, TV, radio, and in person with every conversation you have.

You see, what happens is, beginners start worrying about being grammatically correct, and they quickly become overwhelmed with the fear of: "What if my superlative, pronoun is being used as the present participle?"

The plain truth is, the written word is simply communication. You know, they're reading from scripts in movies and TV shows, even live sporting events have scripted sections, and a plan for the broadcast, come on man!

Here's the deal, it really doesn't matter if you're writing with a dangling participle, over a postmodifier, and your action verbs, agree or not. The age old advice is to write the way you talk, and it's true.

If you really dig in and discover who your reader is, you'll connect with him. And if your just talking with him, having an intimate conversation, he's not going to give a quivering fart about your predicate dangling modifier verbs agreeing.

In my line of work, I have to sell, sell, and sell through the written word. I'm a salesman sitting behind a typewriter. My talent, skill, and abilities directly correspond to my income. Let me tell you, becoming a good writer doesn't just happen overnight, it's not an accident, and prose doesn't just come outpouring, when you set fingers to a keyboard.

The basics of effective writing are a combination of three things: copywriting, continuous learning, and doing. Stephen Kind said: "On writing-a matter of exercise. If you work out with weights for fifteen minutes a day over the course of ten years, you're gonna get muscles. If you write for an hour and a half a day for ten years, you're gonna turn into a good writer."

And here's the deal, if you're feeling as though you lack writing skills, you can't wait ten years, to become a good writer. It's not even like you have to be a good writer, in order to write a good book. If you start today, in ten years, you can always edit and revise your current book, tweak it a little, but in the meantime have royalty payments hitting your bank account, as often as Lebron James makes jump shots.

You see, the only way to become good at anything, is to start badly, and this is your first book. You'll make a few mistakes, but who cares! You're doing it, the guy that has a problem with your participles dangling, probably hasn't written to eat, or maybe written at all, or worse yet, written only for the world of academia. That's not the real world!

Do the best you can, and if you're thinking about it, it's because you care, and want to do a good job. You will, don't worry and be happy, my friend!

John Wooden preached the basics to his basketball teams, he said he would start practices without a basketball. Just picture it, the national championship team is practicing shooting jump shots and dribbling down the court, just one thing, they forgot the basketball. These days, the press would have a field day!

Brian Tracy the author of over 50 books says: "If it's worth doing, it's often worth doing poorly at first, and many times, until you master it." And my favorite is Samuel Johnson's wise advice: "No man but a blockhead writes except for money."

3. Write To One Person

You need to write to just one reader, as in I'm writing to you, right now. Avoid trying to write to all of "them" and instead, picture yourself talking with one, single, solitary person. I like to picture my 3 year old nephew, of course, when he's older.

I do suggest if you can, pick a loved one, because this will help personalize and give your words warmth. It's a good practice to write in the active voice, use short sentences, include contractions, and don't overthink, keep it easy! It's just doing layups, there's no need to shoot three pointers.

4. Attention Span In Our Brave New World

Let me ask you, when do you think the following was said:

"People have the attention span of 30 seconds, and thus your had better take full advantage of this 30 seconds, every chance you get."

This is a quote from Milo Frank in his book How To Get Your Point Across In 30 Seconds, and it was said way back in 1986! Surprised? Maybe, but I'm sure you see the truth in this statement, and I'm sure you see, if it was true in the 1980's it must be just as applicable today, with the advent of the internet, so called smart phones, social media, and a million other shiny technology buttons!

You see, with your writing you want to be concise, clear, and get right to the point. Avoid writing to hit a certain length, or word count. Certainly, you've watched a movie, that could've ended 15 minutes earlier. You see, this is a law of entertainment. Always, leave your audience wanting more, not wanting less! Get your point across, and keep moving, avoid beating it into the ground or else you may wind up saying: "Will anyone … anyone buy my book?"

5. Be Different

One of the most common mistakes is trying to copy other good books. With one of my businesses, teaching guys how to talk to women, I teach them, they must be different. For I've yet to date a woman that said: "Gee, shucks Dan, you're just like every other guy, therefore I feel compelled to kiss you."

In your writing you want to "pop through the clutter" and be unique, offer something new, and build upon the existing body of knowledge in your topic. This is what the evolutionists say make human beings, different from other species, such as Neanderthals, the ability to build upon and expand on our knowledge base.

An excellent way to be different is to inject stories in your book. Since the dawn of mankind, we've sat around a fire and told stories to one another. This is how knowledge and information is passed from one generation to the next, and from one person to another.

Include stories from your life, cool stories of celebrities, and relevant applicable stories, this is what good teachers do, be it in high school or sitting in a church pew. The point with stories is to personalize your book, and make it relatable so your reader can connect with you!

6. Be Like Jesus

I grew up in the church the son of a preacher man. I live the gospel of success, but I don't consider myself formally religious. With that said, religion still contains many useful lessons, and one of my favorite comes from The Sermon on the Mount. For in this bible passage, one of the most useful principles is shared:

"When Jesus had ended these sayings, the people were astonished at his teaching, for he taught them as one having authority, and not as the scribes."

A scribe of course is a writer in biblical times. Express yourself, your opinions, your thoughts, and your findings, in your writing, this is your book, make it so! When you write with authority and decisiveness like Jesus, you're simply being confident, assertive, and having personality.

Folks, aren't interested is a second rate version of whoever your copying, just like they aren't interested in watching some guy pretend to be Matt Damon, Tom Cruise, or Will Smith on the big screen. Make your work original and in your voice, your words, and with your style! This will directly translate into how successful your book is.

Step #4 - Wrap Up

You've got to find your voice, and be yourself. Write with authority, and the way you talk. Don't worry about your dangling participles, and if they agree or not. Be kind to yourself, and if you're feeling like your lacking skills, keep writing, that's one surefire way of gaining more skills. Do your best, and you'll write a terrific book, I guarantee it!

Chapter 6. Your Rough Draft

This is the most challenging step, taking your magnificent ideas, and weaving them into majestic words, and tangible sentences. Please, stay calm, cool, and collected.

This is the meat of your book, and the contents. Don't concern yourself here with punctuation, grammar, flow, style, or any details. We will go back through and polish it all up in the future, right now, just write! The time is upon you. You've got nothing to lose, and everything to gain! Earl

Nightingale said: "Ideas are worthless unless we act on them."

Dictate or Type?

You may've heard it's a good idea to dictate or speak your book. There are speech recognition programs, such as Dragon Dictate, and the Mac computer has a tool these days. In addition you can record it, and pay a neighborhood kid, to type it up.

If this works for you, by all means run with it!

I've used speech recognition software, and may again in the future. It could be from years of training, but, writing on a keyboard is my preferred method, at least for my final draft. I'm a student of both schools, but you've got to figure how you work best here, the only wrong choice is not doing anything.

Work From Paper

It's wise to work from paper. In other words, make an outline for the specific chapter, your working on with this assignment. It's useful with organizing your ideas, the sequence, and you may simply want to jot down a few keywords to make sure you've included everything you want in a chapter.

Set Things Aside

If you've only got a working title, no beginning, no ending, no table of contents, yet. Forget it, and just write. Set the details aside, and we'll go back in the editing process. You see, writing a book, is like chiseling a statue from a block of stone, with nothing written, were still waiting to make our first strike, you must start somewhere.

If you've got the urge, to write chapter 6, this week, then start there, just do it! You don't have to write your chapters, in any order, and in this step were really just getting your book out of your head, and out on paper and into words. We can always clean it up and rearrange it later. There are no rules, but you do have to write, just like Michael Jordan had to practice.

One of the life lessons Michael said he wants most to pass along to his kids, is to always expect the best! You should too expect the best for your book, how cool will it be to type your name into iTunes and see your book show up?

Working Environment

A common stumbling block, is your working environment. The plain truth is it's not likely you'll be able to write a great book, if the television is on, your kids are screaming in the background, your responding to text messages, or surfing the internet! I know this is common sense right … BUT, PLEASE … BE SMART!

Do whatever you need to do, to put yourself in place that does not permit any random interruption, like a fart in the wind. You need to focus, and your friend Susan, will still be waiting to tell you about how Becky said her butt looks big.

I've worked from home since 2006, and I don't care if the Pope himself is calling I do not take unscheduled phone calls. I don't believe in instant communication and you must make an appointment with me, even my loved ones, to spend time together.

You see, I've gone to great pains, and effort to live my life, on my schedule and on my terms. Now, I'll admit I may be a bit extreme, but it's what works for me. I do believe there is a plethora of benefits with technology, but if you leave yourself open to let any ole person, stick their finger in your life, you won't be disappointed and constantly interrupted.

Keep The End In Mind

Yes, keep the finish line at the top of your mind. You'll soon be a published author, this is a huge gold star to add to your resume. Along with being able to earn passive, recurring income. Please, keep this anticipation of accomplishment, always in your thoughts. And keep working, to move towards it.

Relax

It is required you stay relaxed in this process. It's so easy to get overwhelmed thinking about all the little details, but it's just one step at time. It does take self discipline. Keep your reasons list handy, and look at it often.

When you're feeling overwhelmed, tense, and anxious those feelings seep through into your writing. It's also how you get sick. William Shakespeare said: "Our doubts are traitors to us, and make us lose the good we oft might win, by fearing to attempt."

It's important you put your personality in your book, and the only way you can do this, is when your calm, cool, collected and enjoying the journey. Be flexible, and listen to yourself. You'll likely need to tweak a few of these ingredients. It does require effort, to write and plan.

When you've got a good plan, the writing process is much easier. I like to picture my ideal reader, or my 3 year old nephew, just waiting for me to write. Your ideal reader, is just waiting for you! Please, write it and write to that one person!

It's said Phil Jackson the head coach of 11 NBA championship teams would have his players, during a timeout, in those precious 30 to 60 seconds, grab a swig a water, and go to that special safe place in their mind and relax. If Phil Jackson said it, Michael Jordan and Kobe Bryant used it, it's good enough for me!

Step #5 - Wrap Up

The time is upon you, cast off the false belief of you can't. John Wooden would say to thee: "Do not let what you cannot do interfere with what you can do." Start now, no more whining, complaining, or excuse making. Make the magic happen, and enjoy the journey. It's kind of like losing your virginity, you'll always remember this time! And if you're still with me here, I'm confident I can say the same to you, that I said to the woman I gave my V card to, thanks for laughing!

Chapter 7. The 8 Strategies To Defeat The Plague of Writer's Block

Writers block is performance anxiety: musicians, celebrities, athletes, and even speakers suffer from it. There are endless reports of authors resorting to substances, such as Edgar Allen Poe, drinking alcohol. But, I'm not a big fan of paying that high of a price, or following in Sigmund Freud's footsteps, let alone suffering from a major illness.

Follow these 8 strategies to defeat the black plague of writer's block, once and for all.

1. Get Away

If you've really got nothing to say or write, go get away. You're in desperate need of a break! And if you can only afford to get away for 15 minutes, GO DO IT! You have to clear your calculator, relax, and stay calm. It's good to use some self discipline to continue moving forward, but be kind to yourself or else you'll be sick!

Go watch a movie, take a walk in the woods, go listen to a lecture, go to the beach, do something out of your normal routine, even just getting some fresh air outside. Clear all the clutter out of your mind and give your brain a break. I've always got a few projects I'm working on, and you'll likely benefit by investing some time, on some other projects. Just give yourself a break.

2. Doubt

One of the big causes for the plague, is doubt, fear, and second guessing yourself. The plain truth is were just choosing a path, there are a million different paths, we just have to choose one path, you must decide, or get off the pot, little miss Sally!

Mentally picture and even visualize yourself as a proficient, authoritative writer, with an abundant supply of words, descriptions, and vocabulary that just roll off your fingers, like a California mud slide on steroids. Paint a masterpiece for your reader, while sharing a positive, uplifting, and encouraging message with him! See and expect yourself to be great, and follow that up with effort, and you will be great!

You may additionally want to try some breathing exercises, relaxation techniques.

The objective is to perform and not worry about what "they" may think. Instead, focus on who you'll help with your information, along with how it will help you.

3. Get New Input

When you're creating, producing, and outputting stories, and information, it's vital to continuously feed your mind new information. The idea is just like a car in need of gasoline, or your body needing food. You have to keep feeding yourself new and fresh material in order to produce good work, no matter what your career.

Have you not heard it said by the super achievers in life, they learn from every experience?

There are many great ways you can continue to feed your mind, but feed it the good stuff. Just like your body, if you feed your mind only junk, it's hard to produce quality work, but we all need a little bit of mindless junk from time to time, just make sure it's not on a regular occurrence.

4. Avoid Perfectionism

I know, it's easy to want your book to be absolutely perfect. But the truth is, once you write a book, it can always be better, this is because you're a better writer for having gone through the journey and writing it in the first place.

Doesn't that make sense?

Leonardo da Vinci is said to have never finished working on the Mona Lisa, in fact he's said to have continued working on this masterpiece, for the next ten years.

This is one reason why, I suggest you wait and write your introduction or beginning after your get the meat of your book out, because you will be a better writer then. It's just like NFL hall of fame quarterback Joe Montana, he worked and put in effort every single year, to become a better player, it didn't just happen. And you'll have to do the same, but you can't wait to play until you're ready for the NFL.

Understand the nerves and butterflies, are normal. It's performing. It's simply part of the process of writing a book and becoming a more skilled writer.

Surely, you've seen 2nd, 3rd, and even the 27th editions of a book? You see, you can always edit, fix, and revise, or totally change it in the future, especially with ebooks today, and self publishing platforms. It's very easy to edit your book, but you must hit publish FIRST ... that's the hard part.

Do your best and I suggest you don't worry about making revisions, or edits until after you've sold a certain number of copies, or have written four more books.

This is the way life works, many folks get stuck on pressing that publish button. Please, don't fall victim to this.

5. Be The Answer

Look, most folks that are looking for help within your topic, are suffering. This is how people myself included learn new skills. You see, if they already knew, they wouldn't be reading your book.

It's a common false belief that you're writing to the experts. You may be, but, this shouldn't be your ideal reader. The guy suffering should be your ideal reader. I know it's cliche, but isn't there a saying about how if you help just one person then it's worth it?

It's up to you if that's going to be true or not, only please, do give yourself a chance to help someone, it's worth it!

6. Avoid Temporary Embarrassment or Desirable Results

You see, you might not write a best selling book. You may not even have one person, buy your book. But let me ask you, would you rather avoid temporary embarrassment or get desirable results?

The truth of the matter, is you may be embarrassed by your writing, and I guarantee you will be if you continue to write. Heck, Earl Nightingale says he can look at his writings from only a few years prior, and can see how much better he's become. You'll get better just like Earl. But, don't be fearful of a little temporary embarrassment, that is the price of desirable results. And you may also publish your book, and have a stampede of folks running to purchase it and it be the next best thing, since sliced bread.

You see there's only one way to find out!

7. Laugh

Go laugh, really we don't do it enough, and when you're feeling good, you're writing good. Please, get some comedy in your life, and laugh at yourself, and go play with some kids, tell them some stories, and just enjoy your life.

Your book is just a book, it's most important to keep life in balance. Often, we all need to lighten up, with ourselves. Check out some Will Ferrell, and Steve Carrel. And avoid watching the news.

I must share this story with you in hopes of creating some laughter. While writing this book I heard an aspiring author say he had to stop watching Fox news because it was making him angry! Ha, my extension would be any news, and all the talking heads on TV! Sheer lunacy!

Your time is MORE IMPORTANT … especially with our so called 24 hour news channels that report "outrage" over the owner of a basketball team being a racist. Come on man, what world do you live? Santa claus, unicorns, and leprechauns, don't exist either!

Stay away from this stuff, it is the forsaken path of productivity! Instead, stay upbeat, feel good, and enjoy the journey, avoid the illness. And have fun!

If it was easy, or positive thinking alone could do it, then everyone would do it. This project is worth it and can provide a plethora of opportunity, go read your reasons list a couple dozen more times.

You see, I heard a preacher say that pain, is necessary to find Jesus, so then wouldn't it only seem reasonable that pain too, is necessary for writing a book.

Good things, are often set, just out of reach to see how committed we are, and how badly you really want it. Keep running, keep pushing, and you'll get there!

8. The Boy Who Couldn't Communicate

We all take life for granted, and the gifts we have. The truth is, there are folks all around us, in tragedy, despair, and hopelessness. One story, of a 12 year old little boy, we'll call Billy.

Billy was an incredibly outgoing, voracious, little guy, until one summer afternoon, he came down with a headache, and had a brain aneurism burst.

Miraculously he survived, in fact it burst again months later in surgery. And the day he woke up after his surgery, he couldn't communicate. He'd lost the skills to talk, write, even walk. He saw an endless line of therapists, spending hours, grunting with wooden tongue depressors in his mouth, trying to write his a, b, c's, and merely walking to the bathroom by himself.

For weeks his little brain was working, but he just couldn't communicate with the outside world. He was trapped, in a looking glass on life! One day in the ICU, Billy wasn't even able to tell his Dad he had to pee, and intentionally wet the bed.

Gone ... communication ... life!

This is a true story, and it's my story. Unlike, many similar stories, I had a seizure about 30 days later, and miraculously the impossible ... once again happened. Everything instantly came back, as quick as you can snap your fingers.

Life is strange, and don't let this chance to help other people, pass you by. It's important to share your knowledge while you have the opportunity.

You've got nothing to lose and a whole life to gain!

Life is meant to be exploited and lived!

Be thankful and grateful for what is right in life. It's not perfect and it will never be, but the cliche saying about how you don't really know what you have till it's gone, is true!

And I'll never forget that day peeing on myself, it's jet fuel to appreciate all the gifts in life.

Step #6 - Wrap Up

It's key to keep your life balanced, take time away, and enjoy this process. Continue to feed good mental meals, to your brain, to assist your writings. Be thankful, and grateful for the opportunity to help other people.

Chapter 8. Length of Your Book

We're living in a brave new publishing world. The length of your book, is much less important than in the past. You see, your book, will be viewed more online, versus a shelf in a brick and mortar store.

Mark Twain's Tale

Let me share a story with you about Mark Twain while he was a regular attendee of church on this Easter Sunday, he found himself sitting among the cold, hard, church pews. To his pleasant surprise, the preacher was delivering a terrific message, and in anticipation of the offering, he dug into his pocket and pulled out four quarters. The pastor kept preaching, and preaching, and preaching, and by the time, the offering finally did come round, Mark's four quarters, had been reduced to one.

Brevity is of value. This fact is true for the 1800's, 1980's, and 21st century. Today, we live in the information age!

• Have you had a similar experience as Mark Twain?

• How about a movie that could have ended 15 minutes sooner?

Surely, you've talked with someone and wanted them to JUST GET ON WITH IT!

Your objective is to share your message with clarity, coherently, and concisely. Don't go writing to hit a certain word count, or page number.

The Hollywood Rule

In Hollywood, you always want to leave your audience, wanting more! You never want to leave them wanting less.

Have you seen a Ted Talk?

It's a conference held annually by the non profit, Sapling Foundation. They invite noteworthy speakers to present, it's worth checking out if you've, yet to see one.

Did you know these speakers are limited to 18 minutes?

Granted, your book isn't a speech, but the point here still applies. The truth is, any subject, can be written and talked about for DAYS, heck even years, especially with some of the long winded folks in our families!

Here's the deal, when you're writing to hit a certain number of words, or pages, you're not thinking about your audience. Instead, you're thinking about you. But, this book is written for your reader and not for you. Speak to him!

Avoid This Deadly Sin

A colleague who is an expert in his field, committed this deadly sin in his book. It's 300 pages, but the last 100 pages, are just filler material. He droned on and on, and at one point in his book, he wrote pages of nothing more than quotes about a subject he's not an expert in.

A handful of his readers are, including myself. And the bad part is his "experts" advice is antiquated, and irrelevant, as of today.

If you start rambling on especially about information that your not knowledgeable about, you lose credibility, even if you tell your reader, you're not an expert, like this author did. Instead, just don't include it.

I would recommend you grab this author's book, if it was a 100 pages shorter. It's a good idea instead, to grab a copy of Milo Frank's book How To Get Your Point Across In 30 Seconds or Less, and others.

How Long Then ...

The easy answer is, as long as it takes to say what it is you've got to say. In other words, give your reader your message. Don't intentionally shorten it, but also avoid intentionally lengthening it.

Respect your reader and his time. Avoid second guessing yourself. The reason my colleague added an extra 100 pages, is because he was doubting his work, and felt inadequate with only 200 pages.

This is an antiquated strategy, that was used in the days of the past, with real tangible, books. The fact is with publishing you can make any message fit a number of pages, for the shelf appeal. But today more books are purchased electronically.

Your purpose is to create a message, entertain, and avoid be boring. It's the deadly communication sin of print, TV, on the radio, on the stage. Keep in mind, your readers attention span, along with how it's more fun to think about sex and money, for us all.

Step #7 - Wrap Up

In the 21st century, the idea of hitting a certain length is antiquated. Instead, focus on the content of your message. Write for understanding, clarity, and brevity. Keep your reader entertained, to keep them flipping the pages.

Chapter 9. Clean Up Your Manuscript

In this step were going to start polishing up your book and getting it ready for the presses, it's smart to take a break, before you start here.

The first thing we want to do is print up your manuscript. Once, you have this, you next want to go through it, and make sure you have all your information in the sequence, and order you want to present it.

This includes each specific chapter, and the big picture of your whole book manuscript.

Remember, it's about choosing a path, and not about choosing the right path. The fact of the matter is, you can write a book, any million of different ways, but you've got to choose one way, to publish it, and that's our primary big picture objective.

The mission in this first edit, is to make sure you have all the information you want to include, along with the sequencing of events. You'll likely have to take a pair of scissors, and cut and paste different sections, and items in your book. This is normal, and just part of the process.

Rewrites

Look, movie scripts, books, and all communications undergo rewrites. This is reviewing the exact wording, and making sure your message is being shared most effectively. In this step, you'll be tweaking many of your sentences, paragraphs, and really putting the polish on your work.

You'll likely find some ideas, and concepts you've repeated. From time to time this is okay, but you'll want to focus on clarity, and being concise with your manuscript. The priority is for your reader, to feel like the two of you, are age old pals, lounging on the sofa, having a private conversation. This is an ingredient every good book has in common that enables it to connect with readers.

It's of tremendous value to read your book out-loud. It's invaluable to finding the sections in need of some real polishing.

Get Tough

This is where many folks fold, and continue down the road of merely dreaming of writing a book. You see, the time has come to boil down your message, and get a finished product together. Don't stress it, because you can always change and revise your book in the future!

First, we've got to cross the finish line, and publish it.

Did you know most authors write two, three, sometimes, 12 books, in order to produce and publish one?

This is the result of trying to write a perfect book. But, even when you win the Super Bowl, an Oscar, and sell 20 million copies of an album, these spectacular achievements can always be better! This is a fact of life, nothing anyone, ever does, is perfect, but it sure is good enough to be the best in the world!

You'll need to find a good enough point. You'll have to choose exactly where this is for you. Please, use caution and avoid writing 12 manuscripts to produce one book. You've got to play in the game at some point, and stop practicing.

You see Michael Jackson, became one of the greatest musicians by performing, but I guarantee you, every song he created and published, could've been better, if only by his own standards!

Get Feedback

One of the rookie mistakes is to get "constructive criticism" on your manuscript from your friends, colleagues, and family members.

Why?

First, they're not likely to be your ideal reader. Second, most folks will look enviously upon you, and your work. It's a strange world, and some people find it easier to condemn, criticize, and try to drag you down, rather than produce their own work. You can hear musicians talking about it all the time, and the hip hoppers, say these folks are the "haters."

Many rookie authors, are simply wanting a pat on the back and to hear:

"Kudos, a job well done!"

Listen, I'm giving you kudos, over and over again, because it's a FANTASTIC JOB, WELL DONE! You're one of the few individuals, to follow through, and you're just steps away from becoming a published author, with a good chance to earn passive recurring income, in book royalties! GREAT JOB!

You may want to get professional help with the editing step, and outsource some of this work, or even hire someone to do the editing process on your behalf. If you go down this road, I suggest you check out elance.com. My firm also offers some packages, for editing, marketing, and publishing, full details at DanMoskelUniversity.com, but were a premium priced alternative, primarily used by entrepreneurs, with a full time career.

Look the bottom line, is you've just created something from nothing, how cool is that? Let your sales, and royalty payments, be your feedback instead of your friend Tammy patting you on the back, and then telling you about how Becky said her butt looks big.

Caution

Plan time away, and take some breaks, or else your manuscript will start running together, and you'll become overwhelmed, quickly. We must keep this process simple, easy, and bite sized.

Step #8 - Wrap Up

In this step, were starting to see your manuscript take shape, and polishing it up. This is a big job, and it's wise to plan a few days off, before you start this step. This is about tweaking and checking to make sure you've got everything you want to say about a topic, and said it, how you want to say it.

Chapter 10. Write The Introduction

The introduction of your book is the lead in for your message. You'll want to use this as your preface, chapter 1, or introduction. In addition to using it as your book description.

The objective in this step is to create a sales letter. You see, the title gets your readers attention, then the introduction is what catches your reader, and convinces him to purchase your book.

It's exactly like a two minute movie preview. You want to stick, your best information up front. All the action, all the juicy stuff. This is what your reader, will often base his purchasing decision upon.

It's like the radio single for a music album. Put the best stuff, upfront, and the information that is of most importance to your reader.

You see, people purchase things to solve problems, even to solve boredom. Think about it, would someone purchase a book about ADD, if they weren't suffering from this disorder or didn't have a loved one with it? The answer is NO!

The idea here is to speak to your reader, along with separating yourself from the other books available. Let me share an example with you from a spectacular book by Roger Ailes titled You Are The Message.

The very first chapter, in the first paragraph Roger talks about interviewing Charles Manson, and that certainly hooks you in! Your goal is for your reader to want more, and they can get it, simply by purchasing your book.

If you're a novice to selling, the formula is AIDA: attention, interest, desire, and action. The action of course is purchasing your book. You see, there are likely a number of books about your topic. The introduction is where, you want to really sell your reader, that you have the answers, and your information is the best available.

There is a motivating sequence, but it's good to stay focused on the basics. This includes, speaking directly to one reader, speaking his language, and showing him how your information will solve his problems, along with the transformation it will provide his life, how will his life change? The benefits?

Look, people look for religion, along with products, and services to change and transform their life. If you're dealing with ADD and have no problems, you're not likely to be buying books about that topic. However, if you're hoping to change, and improve life even searching for ways to get better, then you're looking for help. This change and transformation is the real selling points of every product.

• How will your readers life change from your message?
• What is the benefit for your reader to purchase, and read your material?

• What would you say to a friend to convince him you've got the answers he's looking for?

Your book isn't written for you, it's written for your reader to benefit, even if it's simply to be entertained. This is why people go to the movies. Entertainment, it is a fundamental in everything fun and exciting in life. We buy things to solve problems, if there wasn't a problem, no one would ever buy anything!

Focus of the transformational value, your information will provide your reader. Give him your best information first, and really seduce him into wanting more of what your message is offering!

Acknowledgments

You've likely seen an acknowledgments page, or dedication page. If you want to include one in your book, this goes upfront. I'm not personally a fan of acknowledging folks, with the exception of you, the reader.

This is more for ego, and vanity, in my humble opinion. A book is created to help your reader, and your reader, isn't all that interested with who specifically in your family you're dedicating your book too. And without a reader, your book, only collects dust.

About The Author

This is where you'll get a chance to brag. It's very wise, to include an about the author page, and in this section talk about how wonderful you are! Tell your reader where they can get more from you, visit your website, subscribe to your newsletter, check you out on YouTube, follow you on social media. Be somebody!

If you've got a small business, and have created a book, to sell your services and products, include a toll free phone number, offer your reader something of value, such as a free consultation. The objective is to engage and connect with you beyond just a one time or even a one night experience.

View it as an opportunity to develop and cultivate a relationship, it is an opportunity!

And in that spirit, let me ask you to visit DanMoskelUniversity.com and sign up for your free report about how to market your upcoming book.

Step #9 - Wrap Up

In this step, were creating the hook, and movie preview for your manuscript, so we can create a stampede of book royalties to your bank account. Include the best, juiciest, and most important information to your reader, and put it up front, so you can convince him to buy your book. Also create your About The Author page.

Chapter 11. Create an Attention Getting Title

The title of your book is the first thing people see. It will create a first impression with your reader, it's exactly like a headline for an advertisement. You see, you want your title to pop through the clutter, and get your target readers attention. Using our earlier example with Adult ADD, an effective title could be:

- Adult ADD - Dealing and Coping with Distractions
  - How To Deal with Adult ADD
  - ADD - The Essential Guide for Adults

You see, you can accept anyone's money, but you really want to speak to that smaller segment of the market, rather than try and speak to everyone.

<u>Does this make sense?</u>

Be careful not to overthink this step. Your book will be discovered if you do a good job with it, along with the introduction and book description. This is the information that potential readers will see, and make their decision to buy your book, or not, based upon.

Keyword Rich

Please, use a keyword rich title. The idea, is to put your book in good positioning to help you get additional views, and readers. For instance, with our example title, Adult ADD - Dealing and Coping with Distractions, the keyword "Adult ADD" is what were targeting and therefore we should include that word in the title, this is using information from step #2, and building your swipe file, the Google Keyword Tool.

You see, the keywords people type into Google, are also the keywords they type into the Amazon search bar, along with other book retailers. You can drive additional purchases by positioning your book, to show up, when folks search at the book retailers for keyword terms. The higher searches you see for a term, in the Google Keyword Planner, the better, it is to use it in your title. If you'd like to see a video of this process visit DanMoskelUniversity.com and sign up.

This also ensures that your potential reader, knows exactly what it is they're getting with your book. No surprises. You can be creative, and you don't necessarily have to follow this principle, but it's a good idea. After all how on earth would your reader, know what your book is about, if you don't tell it to them, in the title?

Table of Contents

Your table of contents, will also be a frequently viewed item, and is relevant in the buying decision for potential readers. Invest a few minutes and think about how you judge books, and what information you look at, when making your buying decision.

The purpose with this step is to speak your readers language. For example, with my book about email marketing, some of the frequently searched keyword terms, according to the Goggle Keyword Planner include:

- Email marketing campaign
- How to build an email list
- Email marketing examples

The idea is simply to use some chapter titles, that speak more relevantly to your potential reader. You see, if you've got chapter titles that include his most recent 5 Google searches, he's more likely to feel like your book has the answers, he's looking for.

You'll also benefit using some intuition, into what his top concerns within your topic are. With the Adult ADD example, it's likely medication, strategies for dealing with distractions, techniques to stay focused and clear your mind, among others. The more you understand and speak to your reader and his concerns, the more likely you're to sell your book to him.

Please, avoid having over 30 chapters. If you've got more than 30 chapters, it's a good plan to combine a few, or create two books. You see, people will judge your book upon the table of contents, and one of my colleagues wrote a terrific book, but it's got 60 chapters!

For no other reason, than your readers perception avoid having 60 chapters! What on earth! It reminds me of a story I heard a preacher share with me, he was once asked how he became such a good minister, and he replied he read the Bible and prayed everyday. You see, there was a bishop in the room with him, and he said "WHAT, how can you read that thing more than once."

Listen, The Bible intimidates people because of it's size, and number of books.

This same principle applies to your book. Keep the chapters under 30, or write two books.

Readability

This idea is also applicable to the appearance of your material. The objective here is to put some headlines, into your chapters. Break up your information, it will make your material appear more user friendly, than a big block of straight text. You want it to engage your reader, not intimidate him!

It's a good practice to include headers, sub headers, short paragraphs, short sentences, bulleted, and numbered lists. This purpose is to make it easy for someone to read, and consume your book. By the way, The Bible has finally adopted this practice and is now offering versions in paragraph form, instead of 10,000 pages of straight text, which always caused myself to feel overwhelmed trying to read!

Step #10 - Wrap Up

In this step, you want to choose a compelling title that grabs your ideal readers attention. Along with making your manuscript user friendly, with a reasonable number of chapters. Avoid authoring The Bible.

Chapter 12. Final Manuscript

Look, at this stage you've had the opportunity to really clean up your initial rough draft, and should be preparing to go to the presses! In this very last step, you'll want to print up your final manuscript and go thru it one last time.

It's genius to read it out loud. This way you'll have a last check to see if it's written in a friendly conversational tone, and the way we talk, along with checking any grammatical and spelling errors.

Please, make sure that your book is written to your reader. Avoid excessively talking about yourself, and using "I" as this is a frequent stumbling block for many new authors. Your book, needs to be written to your reader, it's not your book, it's your reader's book.

You'll always be able to find places you can make it better, but you'll have to discover a good enough point, for your final version. You see, Joe Montana could always have played better, but the only way he was able to win four Super Bowls, was by getting on the field and putting himself in a position to see good things happen. This principle is equally true for your book, publish the darn thing! You'll always be able to revise and publish an updated version, nothing is locked in forever!

Give Yourself a Gold Star

Listen, there are many folks that dream of writing a book, but you my friend have done it! WAY TO GO! This is a massive accomplishment, please, kick up your heels and enjoy it! Congratulations! You're of the 1%'ers!

Let The World Know About Your Book

Now, comes the fun part. The last step in the process is to let the world know about your new book. If you've done a good job, with positioning it, you'll likely generate some initial sales, but you're always going to need to do some marketing work. This is my forte!

And as a special bonus gift, I'd like to help you. If you reach out to me, once your book is published, (yourself or with a 3rd party company) I'd like to interview you and share it in hopes of generating some sales, along with improving the positioning of your book. You can contact me at dmoskel@gmail.com, and we can schedule a time for this. Limited, to the first 1,000 respondents.

We've also created a free report, that outlines, and goes into specific detail about the tools we use to market our books, and how you can use these too, even if you're a non tech person, and wrote your manuscript with an old school typewriter. Including: email marketing, social media, video marketing, audio book production, and more. To grab this report visit Danmoskeluniversity.com. If you hit some potholes, and need some help changing a tire, please, let us know, were here to help, and we do provide packages for publishing, editing, and even help with ghost writing. And for some folks this may be the right move, I'm not one to judge. In fact, I see the appeal of avoiding the pain and instead just going thru a pre-written book, and saying "yes" that looks good.

Step #11 - Wrap Up

This is the final read, the dress performance, and were off to the publishers. Don't neglect to tell other folks that your book exists. Despite our beliefs, very few folks are waiting to stampede and get it, so we've got to let them know it's there, and they can and should get it.

About The Author Dan Moskel

Dan Moskel wants to help you break free the work money link. He's a self made entrepreneur, and has made it his goal to help others suffering in our Brave New Economy, and stop the days of spending Monday through Friday with coworkers like Dwight Schrute and Michael Scott, from the TV show the The Office. You can connect with Dan on Facebook, Google+, Twitter, and more. Check out videos at Dan Moskel's YouTube channel, and visit our website DanMoskelUniversity.com, for more articles, and to grab your free report.

Other Books By Dan Moskel

Video Marketing For Entrepreneurs

SEO Training Manual - The 10 Golden Steps To Shower In Search Engine Traffic

Email Marketing That Works ... So You Don't Have To

How To Create a Website Easy Button

The Blueprint To Affiliate Marketing

Entrepreneurs Bible to Riches: The Gospel of Wealth Attraction

and.

The Magical Message of Success